MAKING THE
MOST OF THE
BIBLE

JOHN CHAPMAN

MAKING THE
MOST OF THE
BIBLE

JOHN CHAPMAN

 matthiasmedia

Making the Most of the Bible
© Matthias Media 2012

Matthias Media
(St Matthias Press Ltd. ACN 067 558 365)
PO Box 225
Kingsford NSW 2032
Australia
Telephone: (02) 9233 4627; international: +61 2 9233 4627
Email: info@matthiasmedia.com.au
Internet: www.matthiasmedia.com.au

Matthias Media (USA)
Telephone: 330 953 1702; international: +1 330 953 1702
Email: sales@matthiasmedia.com
Internet: www.matthiasmedia.com

ISBN 978 1 921896 80 4

Cover design and typesetting by Lankshear Design.

DEDICATED TO
Len Abbott—
friend, Christian teacher, historian.

Contents

Introduction

DURING MY STAY AT DONALD Robinson Retirement Village, I have been disturbed by the fact that several people who appear in every other way to be disciples of Christ seem only to submit to the Bible's teaching when they agree with it. When they disagree with it, they dismiss it.

This attitude is disturbing to me, as it seems to be exactly the attitude of Adam and Eve in the garden of Eden to the word of God. The evil one asks, "Has God really spoken?" This implies that human beings can decide what God has said and what he hasn't said. They are invited to make themselves the arbiters of God's word, and in effect to become gods themselves. I have always thought that this attitude is the very definition of sin.

When Adam and Eve inform the Serpent that they will surely die if they eat the forbidden fruit, he flatly denies the word of God. He retorts, "You will not surely die". The great tragedy is that they believe this terrible lie, with devastating consequences.

Making the Most of the Bible is designed to help ensure that we don't make the same tragic mistake. The aim of this book is to explore how we know what God has said, with a view to obeying him, and how to read the Bible so that we get the most from it.

John Chapman
September 2012

1 | Faith and the word of God

YOU MAY THINK IT STRANGE that a book about reading the Bible should begin with a chapter about faith. But before we look at how to go about reading the Bible, I thought it would be helpful to think about the nature of the Bible itself, and the nature of faith. This will help us to know what we can expect the Bible to do for us, and how we should approach it. With this in mind, I begin with 'Faith and the word of God'.

The nature of faith

"Without faith it is impossible to please [God]"—so says the writer to the Hebrews (Hebrews 11:6).

Our Lord Jesus says, "If you have faith like a grain of mustard seed, you will say to this mountain, 'Move from here to there,' and it will move" (Matthew 17:20). That really isn't all that much faith—mustard seeds are very small! This has led me to believe that it cannot be our faith itself that is most important, since so little faith is required. No, the most important thing must be the object of our faith: the God who has made such a promise.

In the Old Testament, Elijah prayed that it wouldn't rain, and it didn't rain for nearly four years (1 Kings 17; cf. James 5:17). That is a long time! Elijah's prayers are held up to us as an example of the power of prayer, but he prayed that way because God had told him that it wouldn't rain. So it is not the prayer itself which is powerful, but the promise on which the prayer is based. This is always the way of faith.

Let me illustrate what I am saying. Suppose you are walking in the mountains, and a thick fog—so thick that you can hardly see your hand in front of you—closes in. You know that you should stay put and not proceed, but impatience gets the better of you. As you edge your way along the path, you suddenly slip over the edge and plunge into the gorge below. As luck has it, you manage to grab a small sapling and hang on for dear life. You still can hardly see your hand in front of you, and you start calling out for help. To your immense relief, you hear someone, and suddenly a hand reaches down out of the mist and says, "Hang on to me". You reach out, your hand is grasped tightly, and you are overjoyed. However, do you think you will still be pleased when you discover that on the end of that arm is the mad axeman?! Your faith in this person is totally misplaced. It is of no value at all; indeed, it leads to an even worse situation.

Or consider the supposed 'faith' that asks God for a Mercedes-Benz and then simply believes it will happen. That isn't the Bible's view of faith at all. There is no promise that God will give you whatever you want when you ask in this way! That is wishful thinking, not faith.

So the important thing is not our faith, but the object of our faith, and the promises on which our faith is based.

What is faith?

Perhaps the best definition of faith is seen in the way Abraham trusted God. The Bible tells us that Abraham was "fully convinced that God was able to do what he had promised" (Romans 4:21). God had promised that Abraham's wife Sarah, although well past child-bearing age, would bear him a son. Through that son, God would bless all the nations on earth.

Abraham knew the promise, and he trusted that God would do what he had promised to do. The circumstances surrounding him at the time made no difference to the promise. It was sure and certain. So, against the odds, Abraham continued to trust that God would keep his word, and, in due time, Isaac was born (Genesis 21:1-5). So certain was Abraham that God would honour his promise about this boy, that when God asked him to sacrifice Isaac, Abraham did not hesitate to do so, because he trusted that God would be able to raise him to life again (Genesis 22:1-14; Hebrews 11:17-19).

Abraham's faith in God was so extraordinary that it is highlighted for us as an example that we should all follow.

John's Gospel and belief

Just a glance into the Gospel of John shows that 'faith' (or 'belief') is the way in which the Lord Jesus expects us to respond to him.

John begins his Gospel with a majestic picture of the Lord Jesus Christ. Jesus was in the beginning with God, he is God, and he was the instrument of creation, without whom nothing was made (John 1:1-3). John proceeds to tell us that Jesus came to his own people, but they rejected him. However, if a person does not reject Jesus, but instead receives him—to those who *believe* in his name—he gives the right to become a child of God (John 1:11-12). In this passage, believing in Jesus' name is the same as receiving him. We receive him in the opposite way to which his people rejected him. That is, they did not believe that he was God in the flesh, God the Son.

Trusting Christ is part of responding correctly

Having defined faith (or belief) in this way, we can see that it becomes the standard way for people to respond rightly to Jesus.

John proceeds to tell us about the first miracle which Jesus performed: turning the water into wine at the wedding in Cana of Galilee. John finishes his account of this miracle by telling us that, "his disciples believed in him" (John 2:1-11).

In the next chapter, as Jesus explains the 'new birth' to Nicodemus, he says that, as Moses lifted up the brass snake in the wilderness, "so must the Son of Man be lifted up, that whoever believes in him may have eternal life" (John 3:15). This point is restated again in the following two verses and at the end of the chapter, where believing in the Son is contrasted with rejecting or not obeying the Son, with the added warning that whoever rejects the Son invites God's wrath (John 3:36).

In chapter 4, we read the story of Jesus meeting the Samaritan woman, and her subsequent conversion. Look at the way John emphasizes the importance of believing in the conclusion to this story:

> Many Samaritans from that town believed in him because of the woman's testimony, "He told me all that I ever did". So when the Samaritans came to him, they asked him to stay with them, and he stayed there two days. And many more believed because of his word. They said to the woman, "It is no longer because of what you said that we believe, for we have heard for ourselves, and we know that this is indeed the Saviour of the world". (John 4:39-42)

Having heard Jesus' words, the Samaritans were convinced, and they believed.

This story is followed by the fascinating account of the official whose son is at the point of death. The official asks Jesus to come and heal his son. Jesus tells him to go home, because his son is well. This is how John records the nobleman's reaction:

> The man believed the word that Jesus spoke to him and went on his way. As he was going down, his servants met him and told him that his son was recovering. So he asked them the hour when he began to get better, and they said to him, "Yesterday at the seventh hour the fever left him". The father knew that was the hour when Jesus had said to him, "Your son will live". And he himself believed, and all his household. (John 4:50-53)

At first, the man simply believed Jesus' promise about his son. But the full response came later, when he and his household came to put their trust in the Lord Jesus.

Then in John 6, we read an astonishing claim by Jesus. In response to the question, "What must we do, to be doing the works of God?" Jesus replies, "This is the work of God, that you believe in him whom he has sent" (John 6:28-29).

Again and again, John's Gospel shows that trusting or

believing in the Lord Jesus is the correct way to respond to him (e.g. John 6:47; 7:37-38; 9:35-38; 10:41-42; 11:25; 12:11, 44-46; 17:6-8, 14). Jesus puts himself before us as a person who can be completely trusted. In any and every situation, he is reliable, and will keep his promises. Others may disappoint us, but he will not.

This is why Jesus was so shocked at the way the disciples reacted during the storm at sea (Mark 4:35-41). These men were fisherman by trade, but even they despaired of life, so violent was the storm. Finding Jesus asleep, they woke him with the rebuke, "Do you not care that we are perishing?" Jesus stills the storm with his command, and the disciples are astonished and say, "Who then is this, that even the wind and the sea obey him?"

However, the story doesn't end there. It also includes a stunning rebuke from the Lord Jesus: "Have you still no faith?" he asks them. Jesus expects his disciples to trust him. Indeed, he was not careless of their plight at all. He, the master of the creation, exercises his Lordship and saves them, as he promised he would.

Belief more than mere assent

In English, 'to believe' is often the same as giving assent that certain information is correct. In the language of the New Testament, however, the word 'believe' is much more like our word for 'trust'. The book of James makes this clear. He tells us that even the demons believe in God, and shudder (James 2:19). Little good that belief does them! They don't submit to God or worship him. For James, this is not true faith at all. To believe, or to have faith, means to trust what the Bible says, and to act accordingly.

How faith works

In Hebrews 11, we are presented with many great examples that show us how faith works out in practice in the lives of God's people.

The writer begins by telling us that, "Faith is the assurance of things hoped for, the conviction of things not seen" (Hebrews 11:1). You will see from this that faith is neither 'wishful thinking', nor a 'leap in the dark'. How can the writer be sure of what we hope for? Only because God has told him! Faith is not what happens when there is no information. In fact, there can be no faith without information.

This is illustrated by the example of Noah. He was warned by God of the judgement to come on the human race. Because of this warning, he built an ark, which was the God-given means of saving himself and his family (Hebrews 11:7; cf. Genesis 6:13-22). Without the promise of God and the information it contained, his behaviour would have been totally irrational. With the promise of God, it was thoroughly commendable.

The example of Rahab's faith is interesting. It is said of her that, "By faith Rahab the prostitute did not perish with those who were disobedient, because she had given a friendly welcome to the spies" (Hebrews 11:31; cf. Joshua 6:25). It is salutary to consider what, in fact, she believed. She had no specific promise from God. However, she knew enough about God to realize that resisting him was futile, and she threw her lot in with the people of God. She wanted God to be her God, and she trusted God, who received her even though she did not have a specific promise.

Is it possible to know God and his promises?

Since without faith it is impossible to please God, then with faith it must be possible to know what God is like, what he has promised, and how to please him. This is exactly what the writer of Hebrews tells us.

> Long ago, at many times and in many ways, God spoke to our fathers by the prophets, but in these last days he has spoken to us by his Son, whom he appointed the heir of all things, through whom also he created the world. He is the radiance of the glory of God and the exact imprint of his nature, and he upholds the universe by the word of his power. (Hebrews 1:1-3)

God is a speaking God. He tells us what he is like, what he loves and what he hates. He tells us the way of salvation so we can be forgiven and be at peace with him (Romans 5:1).

What God reveals is truth. It is good for all people, for all times, and in all circumstances. It is not the sort of so-called 'truth' that someone might claim for himself, but that is not necessarily true for others. This is not what the Bible means by truth. In fact, that is a total re-definition of truth. What God has revealed is 'true truth', to use Francis Schaeffer's phrase. It is true for all people, for all time.

This is how the apostle Paul argues. He tells us that Israel's history happened to them, but is recorded for us as an example. What was good for them is good for us as well. It was timeless truth (1 Corinthians 10:11).

For example, it is always wrong to 'bear false witness against your neighbour' (Exodus 20:16). We know this because God has spoken. Not only did God speak this timeless truth, but he wrote it on tablets of stone so there could be no doubt.

Warnings against ignoring God's word

The Bible regularly warns us against not heeding God's word.

> "Today, if you hear his voice,
>> do not harden your hearts, as at Meribah,
>> as on the day at Massah in the wilderness."
>> (Psalm 95:7-8; cf. Hebrews 3:7-8)

Hardening of our hearts against God's word is the opposite of heeding and obeying it. It is the opposite of faith.

Faith is an essential feature of our proper approach to God. It assumes that we can know what God is like, with a view to knowing him and knowing what he has promised to do for us. That is why faith and the word of God are closely linked. Notice how Paul links these features together in Romans 10:

> For there is no distinction between Jew and Greek; for the same Lord is Lord of all, bestowing his riches on all who call on him. For "everyone who calls on the name of the Lord will be saved".
>
> How then will they call on him in whom they have not believed? And how are they to believe in him of whom they have never heard? And how are they to hear without someone preaching? And how are they to preach unless they are sent? As it is written, "How beautiful are the feet of those who preach the good news!" But they have not all obeyed the gospel. For Isaiah says, "Lord, who has believed what he has heard from us?" So faith comes from hearing, and hearing through the word of Christ. (Romans 10:12-17)

2 | Jesus' view of the Old Testament

LIKE EVERY OTHER GODLY MAN of his time, Jesus believed the Old Testament was the words that God had spoken. Sometimes God spoke directly, as with Moses on Mount Sinai. Sometimes he spoke through the prophets, who declared, "Thus says the LORD", or, "the word of the LORD came to me, saying…" The phrase, "our father David, your servant, said by the Holy Spirit…" (Acts 4:25), shows the high place in which God's people held the Old Testament Scriptures.

During a controversy with the Pharisees about whether divorce is permissible, Jesus quotes from Genesis 2 with this statement:

> He answered, "Have you not read that he who created them from the beginning made them male and female, and said, 'Therefore a man shall leave his father and mother and hold fast to his wife, and the two shall become one flesh'?" (Matthew 19:4-5)

Notice that Jesus attributes the words, "Therefore…" to God himself. However, when we go back to Genesis 2:24, we discover that they are an editorial comment by the writer of Genesis. For Jesus, the words of Scripture are the words of God.

Like the godly man in the psalms, Jesus mediated on

the law of the LORD... day and night (Psalm 1:2). He was able to echo the words of the psalmist:

> Blessed are those whose way is blameless,
>   who walk in the law of the LORD!
> Blessed are those who keep his testimonies,
>   who seek him with their whole heart. (Psalm 119:1-2)

The pattern for his ministry

But Jesus didn't just believe that the words of the Old Testament were the words of God. He and his disciples also saw in its pages the pattern for his own ministry.

When Jesus was baptized, the voice of God was heard to say, "This is my beloved Son, with whom I am well pleased" (Matthew 3:17). These words are a quote from the Old Testament to show that Jesus is both the Messiah and the suffering servant of God. To those present who knew their Bibles, they would have recognized the first part of the quote to be a reference to Psalm 2, where God calls the king of Israel "my Son" (Psalm 2:7). This psalm says that God's Messiah will subdue all God's enemies, and rule over all the nations of the earth. The second half of the statement refers to the suffering servant of Isaiah, who is described as the one "with whom [God is] well pleased" (Isaiah 42:1). This servant goes on to bear away the sins of God's people (Isaiah 53).

Matthew then tells us that Jesus was led by the Spirit of God into the desert, to be tempted by the devil (Matthew 4:1-11). Having fasted for 40 days, he was hungry. The devil insinuated that Jesus might not be the Messiah, and that it would be wise to 'run a test' to make sure. This temptation to doubt the word of God is as old as the garden of Eden (Genesis 3:1-3). So Jesus is tempted to change stones into bread, to throw himself down from the pinnacle of the Temple, and to worship Satan himself.

On each occasion, Jesus counters the temptation with a quote from Deuteronomy. Jesus sees his temptation as a parallel with Israel's wilderness wanderings in the Old Testament. After God had brought Israel out from Egypt, they journey to the Promised Land. During this time, they were tested by God. But where Israel failed miserably and succumbed to temptation, Jesus resists temptation with quotes from the Bible, introducing them with the phrase "it is written" (Matthew 4:4, 7, 10). For Jesus, this expression was equivalent to saying, "God has spoken".

The Law and the prophets

Since Jesus was the God-man, we might have expected him to have corrected any part of the Old Testament with which he didn't agree. However, this is not the case. He saw himself as the fulfiller of Scripture, and certainly not its corrector. Look at what he says in Matthew 5:17-18:

> "Do not think that I have come to abolish the Law or the Prophets; I have not come to abolish them but to fulfil them. For truly, I say to you, until heaven and earth pass away, not an iota, not a dot, will pass from the Law until all is accomplished."

This is a very high view of the Scriptures. Notice how Matthew then goes on to describe Jesus' healing ministry as a fulfilment of the Old Testament:

> That evening they brought to him many who were oppressed by demons, and he cast out the spirits with a

word and healed all who were sick. This was to fulfil what was spoken by the prophet Isaiah: "He took our illnesses and bore our diseases". (Matthew 8:16-17; cf. Isaiah 53:4)

In the synagogue at Nazareth, Jesus read another passage from Isaiah (Isaiah 61:1-2; cf. 58:6), and then said to the assembled people, "Today this Scripture has been fulfilled in your hearing" (Luke 4:16-21). He was claiming to be the one to whom this key Old Testament prophecy was referring. Before his death, he said to the disciples, "See, we are going up to Jerusalem, and everything that is written about the Son of Man by the prophets will be accomplished" (Luke 18:31). Then, after his resurrection from the dead, this is how Jesus explains his life and ministry to his disciples:

> "These are my words that I spoke to you while I was still with you, that everything written about me in the Law of Moses and the Prophets and the Psalms must be fulfilled." Then he opened their minds to understand the Scriptures. (Luke 24:44-45)

Mistakes?

Before going any further, it is worth thinking about a question that people often raise about the Bible. For many, the idea that the Bible could possibly be the word of God seems to fly in the face of its human authorship. They argue that the Bible is written by humans, and, because humans make mistakes, there must be mistakes in the Bible.

At first reading, this reasoning seems valid. However, on reflection, it does not necessarily have to be so. Humans don't only make mistakes. Sometimes they make statements that are correct. It is therefore possible—under the power of the Holy Spirit—to make correct statements which convey the full message of God. This is in fact what the Bible says happened. Ponder this passage from 2 Peter:

> And we have the prophetic word more fully confirmed, to which you will do well to pay attention as to a lamp shining in a dark place, until the day dawns and the morning star rises in your hearts, knowing this first of all, that no prophecy of Scripture comes from someone's own interpretation. For no prophecy was ever produced by the will of man, but men spoke from God as they were carried along by the Holy Spirit. (2 Peter 1:19-21)

Do you see what Peter is saying? If the Bible had been written merely by human authors, it would not be completely trustworthy. But the human authors were "carried along" by the Holy Spirit. That's why the Bible is totally reliable and free from mistakes.

What does the Bible claim to be able to do for us?

But if the Bible is God's word, and is reliable, what does it do? What should we expect as we read it? In 2 Timothy 3, there is a clear statement of what we can expect the Bible to do for us:

> But as for you, continue in what you have learned and have firmly believed, knowing from whom you learned it and how from childhood you have been acquainted with the sacred writings, which are able to make you wise for salvation through faith in Christ Jesus. All Scripture is breathed out by God and profitable for teaching, for

reproof, for correction, and for training in righteousness, that the man of God may be complete, equipped for every good work. (2 Timothy 3:14-17)

Since God 'breathed out' the Scriptures, they are profitable to teach us, reprove us, correct us, and train us in righteousness. That is the Bible's aim. It would be totally unfair to expect it to be something other than it claims to be. That is, it is not claiming to be a scientific textbook. Nor will it tell you how to get rich quickly—but it will tell you how to conduct yourself should this happen! Within the confines of its aims, it is reliable. It will not lead us astray. It is unreasonable to ask it to do more than it claims to do.

What does it mean to be a disciple of Jesus Christ?

Since Jesus believed that the Old Testament was the word of God, should those who claim to be his followers not do the same? Do you think we are at liberty to pick and choose which of Jesus' views we will adopt and which we will reject? Even if we were—and I, for one, do not believe this to be the case—by what yard stick would we make such a decision? Wouldn't that put us straight back in the garden of Eden, where all our problems began when the man and the woman were led to believe that they could decide what God had and had not said? Like Jesus, we should listen to—and live by—"every word that comes from the mouth of God" (Matthew 4:4).

3 | Jesus and his words

BEFORE LOOKING FURTHER at Jesus' attitude to the Scriptures, it would be useful to remind ourselves who Jesus is, what the Bible has to say about him, and how we should regard his words.

The New Testament contains some classic statements that reveal the person of Jesus, such as the passage from Hebrews that we first saw in chapter 1:

> Long ago, at many times and in many ways, God spoke to our fathers by the prophets, but in these last days he has spoken to us by his Son, whom he appointed the heir of all things, through whom also he created the world. He is the radiance of the glory of God and the exact imprint of his nature, and he upholds the universe by the word of his power. After making purification for sins, he sat down at the right hand of the Majesty on high. (Hebrews 1:1-3)

Notice that the writer says that Jesus is the exact representation of God. When God chose to reveal himself to us, he did so in the person of his Son. I may talk to you about my brother Jim, but nothing would replace a meeting with him. You would then be able to say, "We heard from you, John, but now we know Jim, because we have met him!" In the same way, now that Jesus has come, we have seen God.

The Apostle Paul describes Jesus in the following way:

> He is the image of the invisible God, the firstborn of all creation. For by him all things were created, in heaven and on earth, visible and invisible, whether thrones or dominions or rulers or authorities—all things were created through him and for him. And he is before all things, and in him all things hold together. And he is the head of the body, the church. He is the beginning, the firstborn from the dead, that in everything he might be preeminent. For in him all the fullness of God was pleased to dwell, and through him to reconcile to himself all things, whether on earth or in heaven, making peace by the blood of his cross. (Colossians 1:15-20)

Paul tells us that all of God's fullness dwelt in Jesus. There was nothing about God the Father which could not be perceived in the person of the Lord Jesus.

Jesus' works and words are one

When, at the Last Supper, Philip says to Jesus, "Lord, show us the Father, and it is enough for us", Jesus answers him:

> "Have I been with you so long, and you still do not know me, Philip? Whoever has seen me has seen the Father. How can you say, 'Show us the Father'? Do you not believe that I am in the Father and the Father is in me? The words that I say to you I do not speak on my own authority, but the Father who dwells in me does his works." (John 14:9-10)

It stands to reason, given the person of the Lord Jesus Christ, that his words must be the words of God. Indeed, he claims that he received them from the Father. It is a great mistake to separate Jesus from his words or his works. They are one and the same. It would be ridiculous to say, "I admire the person of Jesus, but I just wish he didn't say the things he did!" This is to imagine another Jesus from the one we have in the pages of the Scriptures.

The person of the Lord Jesus, his words and his works, tell us exactly what the Father is like. Furthermore, Jesus believes that our response to his words and works will condemn us or excuse us on the Day of Judgement (Matthew 11:20-24; Mark 8:38). So significant are the teachings of Jesus, that he believed that following his teaching would bring stability in life and the ability to withstand the final judgement of God (Matthew 7:24-29).

When Peter, James and John were with Jesus at the Transfiguration, they witnessed firsthand the glory of the Lord Jesus. It was awe-inspiring. We are told that they were so overwhelmed that they didn't know what to say. But God knew what to say: "A bright cloud overshadowed them, and a voice from the cloud said, 'This is my beloved Son, with whom I am well pleased; listen to him'" (Matthew 17:5). The Son is to be taken very seriously. He has the words of eternal life, and to bypass or ignore him is to invite disaster.

Jesus' words are powerful

Jesus' words are extremely powerful. His teachings were unlike those of the scribes and teachers of the law, because they came with such authority (e.g. Matthew 7:29; Mark 1:22). When he exorcized the evil spirit from a man at the synagogue in Capernaum, "[the people] were all amazed and said to one another, 'What is this word? For with authority and power he commands the unclean spirits, and they come out!'" (Luke 4:36)

On another occasion, a centurion sent a message to Jesus with a request to come and heal his slave. Jesus agreed to do so, but as he approached the house, the centurion sent another message:

> "Lord, do not trouble yourself, for I am not worthy to have you come under my roof. Therefore I did not presume to come to you. But say the word, and let my servant be healed. For I too am a man set under authority, with soldiers under me: and I say to one, 'Go', and he goes; and to another, 'Come', and he comes; and to my servant, 'Do this', and he does it." When Jesus heard these things, he marveled at him, and turning to the crowd that followed him, said, "I tell you, not even in Israel have I found such faith". (Luke 7:6-9)

This centurion is used to wielding authority. Yet he is completely willing to submit to Jesus' authority, and he takes him at his word. No wonder Jesus is impressed with this man's faith. However, what matters is not just the man's faith, but the object of his faith: Jesus' power and authority. Jesus simply speaks the word, and the servant is healed.

Remember the incident we examined in chapter 1 when a furious windstorm arose at sea, and the disciples feared for their lives. Jesus commanded the wind and the waves to stop, and we are told that there was such a great calm that they said to each other, "Who then is this, that even the wind and the sea obey him?" (Mark 4:35-41). Whichever way you look at this story, it is very powerful speaking!

Do not be ashamed of Jesus' words

Listen to this saying of Jesus, and the warning he gives to us:

> "Whoever would save his life will lose it, but whoever loses his life for my sake will save it. For what does it profit a man if he gains the whole world and loses or forfeits himself? For whoever is ashamed of me and of my words, of him will the Son of Man be ashamed when he comes in his glory and the glory of the Father and of the holy angels." (Luke 9:24-26)

Such a strong warning only needs to be given if we are under a real temptation to be ashamed of Jesus' teaching. Some people are scandalized by the exclusive claims of the Lord Jesus. For example, in John 14, Jesus says, "I am the way, and the truth, and the life. No one comes to the Father except through me" (John 14:6). Sayings like this seem to be so much at odds with the spirit of our age. Other people take offence at Jesus' teaching about hell and judgement (e.g. Luke 12:1-7).

However, let us remind ourselves again that we cannot extricate Jesus' words from his person. If we acknowledge him as Lord, we must be committed to all of his teachings, not just the parts that are safe or convenient.

The Father gave the words to the Son

In his prayer for the apostles, recorded in John 17, Jesus says:

> "I have manifested your name to the people whom you gave me out of the world. Yours they were, and you gave them to me, and they have kept your word. Now they know that everything that you have given me is from you. For I have given them the words that you gave me, and they have received them and have come to know in

truth that I came from you; and they have believed that you sent me. I am praying for them. I am not praying for the world but for those whom you have given me, for they are yours. All mine are yours, and yours are mine, and I am glorified in them. And I am no longer in the world, but they are in the world, and I am coming to you. Holy Father, keep them in your name, which you have given me, that they may be one, even as we are one. While I was with them, I kept them in your name, which you have given me. I have guarded them, and not one of them has been lost except the son of destruction, that the Scripture might be fulfilled. (John 17:6-12)

Notice how Jesus describes the message which he delivered to the apostles from the Father. It was not simply a generalized message, but was highly specific: "I have given them *the words that you gave me*, and they have received them". It is a clear and specific message, direct from God. And it is by believing these words that we, too, are saved.

The other reason that we can have immense confidence in the words of Jesus is that he was given the Holy Spirit without measure—without limits (John 3:34). As Jesus and the Father are one, so Jesus and the Holy Spirit are one. Jesus spoke the very words of God as the Spirit of God enabled him to do so.

LET ME CONCLUDE THIS section with this wonderful saying of the Lord Jesus about the importance of hearing and accepting his words:

"Truly, truly, I say to you, whoever hears my word and believes him who sent me has eternal life. He does not come into judgement, but has passed from death to life." (John 5:24)

4 | Jesus' view of the New Testament

NONE OF THE NEW TESTAMENT books were written before Jesus rose from the dead and ascended to heaven. He did not write any of them, nor did he read any of them as we do. However, we must not therefore think that Jesus was uninterested in what was to take place after his ascension and the coming of the Spirit. In fact, there is much that we can learn about Jesus' view of the New Testament.

The Holy Spirit: the teacher of the 12 apostles

When Jesus announced to his disciples that he was going away and that they could not go with him, they were filled with concern (John 14:1ff). Who would be their teacher? It may have occurred to them that they would have been wise to have paid closer attention while he was still with them! No doubt, they began to wonder if they would be able to remember his teaching. However, Jesus assures them that they will not be left as orphans. He will send his Spirit to be with them and to live in them. It is hard for us to imagine the relief it must have been to them when Jesus gave them these promises:

> "These things I have spoken to you while I am still with you. But the Helper, the Holy Spirit, whom the Father

will send in my name, he will teach you all things and bring to your remembrance all that I have said to you. Peace I leave with you; my peace I give to you. Not as the world gives do I give to you. Let not your hearts be troubled, neither let them be afraid." (John 14:25-27)

And again:

"I still have many things to say to you, but you cannot bear them now. When the Spirit of truth comes, he will guide you into all the truth, for he will not speak on his own authority, but whatever he hears he will speak, and he will declare to you the things that are to come. He will glorify me, for he will take what is mine and declare it to you. All that the Father has is mine; therefore I said that he will take what is mine and declare it to you." (John 16:12-15)

Jesus' promise is that the Holy Spirit will lead the apostles into all truth. He has kept this promise. He poured out his Spirit on the apostles at Pentecost (Acts 2:1-4), and then equipped the apostles to write the New Testament books. The Spirit led them into all truth and caused them to remember what Jesus had taught them. Hence, there is no crucial teaching of the Lord Jesus that has been lost.

The apostles would have had these promises in mind when they chose someone to replace Judas (Acts 1:12-26). They looked for a person who had been with them continually from Jesus' baptism onwards, and who had witnessed the resurrection. They chose Matthias. The Spirit caused him to remember the sayings of Jesus, since he too had heard them from the beginning.

Before the end of the first century, there was widespread agreement among Christians about which books were written by the apostles, or which books contained the teaching of the twelve. When the Council of Nicaea met in 325 AD, they discussed—among other matters—which books of the New Testament had certainly been authored by the apostles. They were still close enough to the apostles to recognize the authorship of the twelve, and so affirmed their writings as genuine. They also rejected books over which there was legitimate doubt, including two letters claiming to be by the apostle Paul, which were rejected as known forgeries. But for most of the authentic writings, there had simply been no questions asked: they had always been known to be genuinely from the twelve, and were apostolic in authorship or content.

What about the apostle Paul?

About half of the New Testament was written by the apostle Paul. Originally known as Saul, he was not a follower of the Lord Jesus, and he certainly was not a member of the original apostolic band to whom Jesus made the promise that the Spirit would come and cause them to remember his teachings.

Paul did not become a follower of the Lord Jesus until after Jesus had ascended into heaven. He claimed to have been appointed an apostle to the Gentiles by the risen Jesus on the Damascus road. It will be helpful for us to refresh our minds on what took place on that incredible day:

> But Saul, still breathing threats and murder against the disciples of the Lord, went to the high priest and asked him for letters to the synagogues at Damascus, so that if he found any belonging to the Way, men or women, he might bring them bound to Jerusalem. Now as he went on his way, he approached Damascus, and suddenly a

light from heaven shone around him. And falling to the ground he heard a voice saying to him, "Saul, Saul, why are you persecuting me?" And he said, "Who are you, Lord?" And he said, "I am Jesus, whom you are persecuting. But rise and enter the city, and you will be told what you are to do." The men who were traveling with him stood speechless, hearing the voice but seeing no one. Saul rose from the ground, and although his eyes were opened, he saw nothing. So they led him by the hand and brought him into Damascus. And for three days he was without sight, and neither ate nor drank.

Now there was a disciple at Damascus named Ananias. The Lord said to him in a vision, "Ananias". And he said, "Here I am, Lord". And the Lord said to him, "Rise and go to the street called Straight, and at the house of Judas look for a man of Tarsus named Saul, for behold, he is praying, and he has seen in a vision a man named Ananias come in and lay his hands on him so that he might regain his sight". But Ananias answered, "Lord, I have heard from many about this man, how much evil he has done to your saints at Jerusalem. And here he has authority from the chief priests to bind all who call on your name." But the Lord said to him, "Go, for he is a chosen instrument of mine to carry my name before the Gentiles and kings and the children of Israel. For I will show him how much he must suffer for the sake of my name." (Acts 9:1-16)

Whichever way we look at this man, he is special. I have never seen the risen Jesus in the flesh or in a vision. I have not been chosen and appointed by the risen Jesus to take the gospel to the Gentiles. It is just untrue to say that my opinion is as good as Paul's.

However, it would be equally untrue to say that the churches were always ready to receive him as an apostle. The

Corinthians certainly were unsure of Paul's status. That is one of the main reasons Paul wrote 2 Corinthians: it is his defence to the Corinthian church of his genuine apostleship.

In another of his letters, Galatians, Paul tells us how he came to understand the gospel. He tells us that it came to him through a revelation of Jesus Christ (Galatians 1:12). He was not taught it by any person. If the revelation he received came from the very person whom he thought was under God's curse—namely, Jesus Christ—it meant that this person was, in fact, the Lord of glory. That would have been enough for him to go back to the Old Testament and interpret it 'christologically'—with Jesus at the centre.

Paul may have also received further revelations, but it is important for us to know what he thought had happened to him. There is a long description found in Galatians:

> For I would have you know, brothers, that the gospel that was preached by me is not man's gospel. For I did not receive it from any man, nor was I taught it, but I received it through a revelation of Jesus Christ. For you have heard of my former life in Judaism, how I persecuted the church of God violently and tried to destroy it. And I was advancing in Judaism beyond many of my own age among my people, so extremely zealous was I for the traditions of my fathers. But when he who had set me apart before I was born, and who called me by his grace, was pleased to reveal his Son to me, in order that I might preach him among the Gentiles, I did not immediately consult with anyone; nor did I go up to Jerusalem to those who were apostles before me, but I went away into Arabia, and returned again to Damascus.
>
> Then after three years I went up to Jerusalem to visit Cephas and remained with him fifteen days. But I saw none of the other apostles except James the Lord's brother.

(In what I am writing to you, before God, I do not lie!) Then I went into the regions of Syria and Cilicia. And I was still unknown in person to the churches of Judea that are in Christ. They only were hearing it said, "He who used to persecute us is now preaching the faith he once tried to destroy". And they glorified God because of me.

Then after fourteen years I went up again to Jerusalem with Barnabas, taking Titus along with me. I went up because of a revelation and set before them (though privately before those who seemed influential) the gospel that I proclaim among the Gentiles, in order to make sure I was not running or had not run in vain. But even Titus, who was with me, was not forced to be circumcised, though he was a Greek. Yet because of false brothers secretly brought in—who slipped in to spy out our freedom that we have in Christ Jesus, so that they might bring us into slavery—to them we did not yield in submission even for a moment, so that the truth of the gospel might be preserved for you. And from those who seemed to be influential (what they were makes no difference to me; God shows no partiality)—those, I say, who seemed influential added nothing to me. On the contrary, when they saw that I had been entrusted with the gospel to the uncircumcised, just as Peter had been entrusted with the gospel to the circumcised (for he who worked through Peter for his apostolic ministry to the circumcised worked also through me for mine to the Gentiles), and when James and Cephas and John, who seemed to be pillars, perceived the grace that was given to me, they gave the right hand of fellowship to Barnabas and me, that we should go to the Gentiles and they to the circumcised. Only, they asked us to remember the poor, the very thing I was eager to do. (Galatians 1:11–2:10)

The gospel Paul received by revelation from the Lord Jesus turned out to be exactly the same as the gospel that the apostles had received. This should fill us with great confidence: today, we have received the same gospel. It has come to us from different sources, but each source received it from Jesus himself. That is why Peter is able to refer to Paul's writing as 'Scripture' (2 Peter 3:15-16). It is important for us to realize that the scruples which some have about Paul's writings today were not shared by the other apostles.

We can be confident about the Bible we have received

We can be certain that the Bible we have in our hand is the word of God, and that it is the place to go if you wish to hear God speaking to you.

I once taught a boy who told me that his method of learning his spelling was to put the spelling book under his pillow at night, and to sleep on it. His results showed that this method was totally unreliable! Many people approach God in a similar way. They do not really know what God is like because the method they use is to find him is unsatisfactory. They just don't read his word! Reading the Bible is the normal way to hear God speak. If you wish to hear what God has to say to you, listen to him as he speaks in his word.

However, the Bible is no ordinary book. The word that God has spoken is living and dynamic, and will continue to speak to us today. I have often asked Christian people when they are most conscious of 'being in the presence of God'. Invariably they say, "When I am at prayer". I think I am most conscious of being in the presence of God when I am reading his words—as he speaks to me.

The tragedy of our age is that 'the phone is ringing and ringing'. God has spoken, and he wants us to know what he is like, but we neglect to 'lift the receiver' and listen. We do it to the peril of our souls.

5 | Forgiveness, life after death, and the Bible

Now that we have looked at Jesus' views on the Bible, and the nature of the Bible itself, we will briefly consider the message at the heart of the Bible. That message centres on the forgiveness of sins and the promise of life after death that Jesus offers to us all.

One of the best parts of being a Christian is knowing that we are forgiven by God for our past actions and our rebellious attitudes towards him. It's hard to think of anything more reassuring than the opening statement of Romans 5: "Therefore, since we have been justified by faith, we have peace with God through our Lord Jesus Christ" (v. 1). Or consider the opening words of Romans 8: "There is therefore now no condemnation for those who are in Christ Jesus" (v. 1).

The promise that, one day, I will be welcomed into the presence of God as if I had never sinned fills me with wonder and awe. The idea of being at peace with God is almost too wonderful to believe.

I remember being in the common room of Robb College at the University of New England with a group of young men. I was explaining that being 'justified' means that God treats us as if we had never sinned. One of the men said to me, "Are you saying that God will forget about my past?"

I replied, "That is exactly what I am saying!" The tears welled up in his eyes, and he whispered, "That's nearly too good to be true". "It is, but it happens to be true", I assured him.

I know how he felt! Recently in the chapel I attend at my retirement village, the preacher told us that, when he was in his late teens, he was greatly affected by a sermon he heard. He was asked to envisage his life story being shown for all to see on the coming Day of Judgement. He said he was guilt-stricken at the thought that his mother would see it! I'm sure we can all identify with this experience. I can certainly remember the relief I felt when I realized that I was totally forgiven for all my sins.

Total forgiveness

The Bible has several metaphors to describe this idea. I will list several of them so you can read them easily.

> For as high as the heavens are above the earth,
>> so great is his steadfast love toward those who fear him;
> as far as the east is from the west,
>> so far does he remove our transgressions from us.
> As a father shows compassion to his children,
>> So the LORD shows compassion to those who fear him.
> (Psalm 103:11-13)

God's love for us is infinite. How comforting that idea is! In his infinite love, he has taken our sins an infinite distance from us: as far as the east is from the west. That is a long way!

> He will again have compassion on us;
>> he will tread our iniquities underfoot.
> You will cast all our sins
>> into the depths of the sea. (Micah 7:19)

Notice the graphic ways in which this metaphor depicts the totality of our forgiveness. Our sins are trampled underfoot and cast "into the depths of the sea". They are completely removed from us.

> "And no longer shall each one teach his neighbour and each his brother, saying, 'Know the LORD', for they shall all know me, from the least of them to the greatest, declares the LORD. For I will forgive their iniquity, and I will remember their sin no more." (Jeremiah 31:34)

Can you think or anything better? God promises to forget about my sins.

> Behold, it was for my welfare
>   that I had great bitterness;
> but in love you have delivered my life
>   from the pit of destruction,
> for you have cast all my sins
>   behind your back. (Isaiah 38:17)

Here, the prophet Isaiah tells us of his own experience of God's forgiveness. God puts Isaiah's sins behind his back.

> "I, I am he
>   who blots out your transgressions for my own sake,
>   and I will not remember your sins." (Isaiah 43:25)

God is a forgiving God (cf. Daniel 9:9). He tells us—just as he told Isaiah—that he will remember our sins no more.

Have you noticed that all of these passages are from the Old Testament? I find it so hard to understand those people who claim that the God of the Old Testament is hard and cruel, while the God of the New Testament is kind and loving. I have not found it that way at all. God never changes. We would do well to remember that when the Lord Jesus prayed, "I thank you, Father, Lord of heaven and earth" (Matthew 11:25; Luke 10:21), he was speaking to the same God who is pictured for us in the pages of the Old Testament. Because God never changes, the Old Testament promises of the forgiveness of sins apply to us today.

I think it is wonderful to know that I will not have to answer for my sins—that they have been removed from me as far as the east is from the west. I am still amazed that, on the Day of Judgement, I will be welcomed by God because Jesus has taken the punishment my sins deserve. He has done for me what I could not do for myself. See how this is described by the apostle John:

> Beloved, let us love one another, for love is from God, and whoever loves has been born of God and knows God. Anyone who does not love does not know God, because God is love. In this the love of God was made manifest among us, that God sent his only Son into the world, so that we might live through him. In this is love, not that we have loved God but that he loved us and sent his Son to be the propitiation for our sins. Beloved, if God so loved us, we also ought to love one another. (1 John 4:7-11)

The new creation

While our sins can be forgiven now, the New Testament writers do not believe that we reach our full potential in this age. Like their Old Testament forefathers, they were looking forward to the 'new creation'.

When the Lord Jesus was on the eve of his death, he told his disciples that he was going to prepare a place for them, and that in that place we would be with him forever (John 14:1-2). It is true that the Bible does not give us a complete picture of the new creation, but there are two wonderful poems in Isaiah and a poetic description in Revelation that combine to give a striking depiction of the future. Let us look at each of them in turn.

> ...many peoples shall come, and say:
> "Come, let us go up to the mountain of the LORD,
>> to the house of the God of Jacob,
> that he may teach us his ways
>> and that we may walk in his paths".
> For out of Zion shall go the law,
>> and the word of the LORD from Jerusalem.
> He shall judge between the nations,
>> and shall decide disputes for many peoples;
> and they shall beat their swords into plowshares,
>> and their spears into pruning hooks;
> nation shall not lift up sword against nation,
>> neither shall they learn war any more. (Isaiah 2:3-4)

Our writer envisages a new age. He sees that all the nations will come home to Mount Zion, and to God. God will judge between nations, and there will be no more war.

I have lived most of my life in the 20th century, and I have read some of the letters which were sent home by Australian soldiers who fought in the First World War. They are full of idealism. They talk about how they will rid the world of suffering and injustice. "This war", they said, "will be the war to end all wars". The tragedy is that they really believed it. At least 25 per cent of those soldiers are buried at Flanders and Mons. It is so hard for us to imagine that they believed this— "the war to end all wars"! Alas, it was not to be.

During the 20th century, we lurched from one war to the next. As we enter the 21st century, this looks as if it will continue. That is why it is so good to read that in the new age, people will beat their swords into ploughshares and their spears into pruning hooks. What a world! It sounds almost too good to be true.

There is another beautiful poem in Isaiah about the world to come:

> There shall come forth a shoot from the stump of Jesse,
>   and a branch from his roots shall bear fruit.
> And the Spirit of the LORD shall rest upon him,
>   the Spirit of wisdom and understanding,
>   the Spirit of counsel and might,
>   the Spirit of knowledge and the fear of the LORD.
> And his delight shall be in the fear of the LORD.
> He shall not judge by what his eyes see,
>   or decide disputes by what his ears hear,
> but with righteousness he shall judge the poor,
>   and decide with equity for the meek of the earth;
> and he shall strike the earth with the rod of his mouth,
>   and with the breath of his lips he shall kill the wicked.
> Righteousness shall be the belt of his waist,
>   and faithfulness the belt of his loins.
>
> The wolf shall dwell with the lamb,
>   and the leopard shall lie down with the young goat,
> and the calf and the lion and the fattened calf together;
>   and a little child shall lead them.
> The cow and the bear shall graze;
>   their young shall lie down together;
>   and the lion shall eat straw like the ox.
> The nursing child shall play over the hole of the cobra,
>   and the weaned child shall put his hand on the adder's den.
> They shall not hurt or destroy
>   in all my holy mountain;
> for the earth shall be full of the knowledge of the LORD
>   as the waters cover the sea. (Isaiah 11:1-9)

This wonderful new world will be brought about by the Lord Jesus—the "shoot from the stump of Jesse". He will be its king.

Again, it all sounds too good to be true—like whistling in the dark to keep your spirits up when things look bleak. It would be that way, if it were not for the Lord Jesus and what he has accomplished for us.

Finally, we have a prose-poem in the last book of the Bible, Revelation:

> Then I saw a new heaven and a new earth, for the first heaven and the first earth had passed away, and the sea was no more. And I saw the holy city, new Jerusalem, coming down out of heaven from God, prepared as a bride adorned for her husband. And I heard a loud voice from the throne saying, "Behold, the dwelling place of God is with man. He will dwell with them, and they will be his people, and God himself will be with them as their God. He will wipe away every tear from their eyes, and death shall be no more, neither shall there be mourning, nor crying, nor pain any more, for the former things have passed away." (Revelation 21:1-4)

It is so hard to imagine. No more death! No more parting! No more pain! No more sorrow! God will wipe away all tears from their eyes! Let it roll on!

But is it true? Well, if Jesus is the king of this world and of the world to come, he can certainly do it. The records in the Bible about him, the Gospels, bear witness to his power. He raised the dead, healed the sick, fed the hungry, forgave sins, and opened the eyes of the blind. There is no doubt that he can do it. He has the power, and he will do it, because he has promised to do it.

Is it really true?

Have you notice that every time I want to assert some truth about God and us, I have gone straight to the Bible? This is the only way we can know about the forgiveness that God offers. If it weren't for the promises in the Bible, we would not know that our sins could be dealt with. Thank God that Jesus showed us, by his own attitude to the Bible, that it is a reliable book. It can be trusted completely, because we can trust Jesus (and his attitude towards the Scriptures) completely.

If we cannot trust the Bible, we have no sure hope. We might wistfully hope for some better future, but what good is that? At the end of the day, we would be left without any hope or any sure foundation. But this is not the case. Jesus is totally trustworthy. He calls on us to trust him, and to trust that the words of the Bible are the very words of God. What I have done with 'forgiveness' and the 'new creation' in this chapter could be done with any of the great truths of Christianity. For example, how do you know that God loves you? Because he tells us in the Bible. How do we know that evil will be ultimately judged and overthrown? Because God tells us in the Bible. Those who undermine people's confidence in the Holy Scriptures do so at great peril.

Karl Barth, the great Swiss German theologian of the 20th century, was once asked to summarize the essence of the millions of words he had published. He replied: "Jesus loves me, this I know, for the Bible tells me so".

6 | Reading the Bible for all its worth

THE BIBLE IS NOT A MAGIC BOOK. You can't find out what is in it unless you read it. The first step to getting to know God is to listen to him as he speaks. Find your Bible, and start reading.

What is the Bible?

The Bible consists of 66 books that have been bound together into one book for our convenience. They were written over a long period of time. Thirty-nine of them were written before Jesus was born, and they point us to him. Collectively, these are called the Old Testament. The other 27 were written after Jesus ascended into heaven. They are called the New Testament.

Remember how the epistle to the Hebrews begins:

> Long ago, at many times and in many ways, God spoke to our fathers by the prophets, but in these last days he has spoken to us by his Son, whom he appointed the heir of all things, through whom also he created the world. (Hebrews 1:1-2)

What is so remarkable, given the great variation of the backgrounds of the Bible's authors, is that they all agree with each other on the nature of God, how we are to relate to him, and how he will solve the terrible problem of evil in the world.

When God chose to reveal himself to human kind, he did it progressively. Through the Old Testament, God was preparing us for the great moment when he appeared in the person of the Lord Jesus. The New Testament tells of the life, death, resurrection and ascension of Jesus, and of the beginning of his church as the news of the forgiveness of sins is preached.

Some of the books of the Bible are history, while others are poetry. Some are teaching on how to live the Christian life. When we come to the Bible, it is important for us to work out the sort of literature we are reading, so that we don't take literally what is meant to be figurative, or vice versa. For example, when Wordsworth says in his poem, "I wandered lonely as a cloud, that floats on high o'er dales and hills", no one believes he has actually become a cloud!

The more you read the Bible, the better you will become at distinguishing which types of books are which. Some are easier to work out and understand. For example, the four Gospels are history. They tell us factual information about the Lord Jesus and his life on earth. The letter to the Romans teaches us—in quite a degree of detail—how to get right with God and stay there. The last book of the Bible, Revelation, is known as 'apocalyptic' literature. This is a particular form of writing where poetry, dreams and visions are used to tell the truth. Sometimes it is difficult to be certain of the kind of literature. Here, we must be patient, trust God, and make every effort to work out how to handle it properly.

Perhaps the best known of the Bible's poems is Psalm 23:

The LORD is my shepherd; I shall not want.
    He makes me lie down in green pastures.
He leads me beside still waters.
    He restores my soul.
He leads me in paths of righteousness
    for his name's sake.
Even though I walk through the valley of the shadow of death,
    I will fear no evil,
for you are with me;
    your rod and your staff,
    they comfort me.
You prepare a table before me
    in the presence of my enemies;
you anoint my head with oil;
    my cup overflows.
Surely goodness and mercy shall follow me
    all the days of my life,
and I shall dwell in the house of the LORD
    forever.

Over the years, this poem has been a comfort and an inspiration to thousands who, in times of difficulty, have found great comfort in its ideas. I am happy to admit that I am one of them. We are reassured that God loves us and cares for us. He will guide us through life. He will be with us in death, and after. What a joy!

The same figure of speech is used by the Lord Jesus in John 10, where he describes himself as "the good shepherd" who lays down his life for the sheep (John 10:11). Similar ideas are also present in the great promise which Jesus makes to his disciples at the end of Matthew's Gospel:

Now the eleven disciples went to Galilee, to the mountain to which Jesus had directed them. And when they saw him they worshiped him, but some doubted. And Jesus came and said to them, "All authority in heaven and on earth has been given to me. Go therefore and make disciples of all nations, baptizing them in the name of the Father and of the Son and of the Holy Spirit, teaching them to observe all that I have commanded you. And behold, I am with you always, to the end of the age." (Matthew 28:16-20)

To have Jesus with you all the time is to have everything which is promised in Psalm 23. For some readers, the Matthew passage will have the greatest impact; for others, the most precious text will be Psalm 23. I have always thought that God has been so kind to make himself known to us with such variation. What appeals to us at one stage of our life may not speak so powerfully at another. That is why the important truths in the Bible are stated over and over again—sometimes with one figure of speech, sometimes with another.

Humility is essential

It should go without saying that when we come to the Bible, we should do so with a humble heart which is longing to know what God says, with a view to being obedient. The proud heart is disqualified from knowing the mind of God. Such people cannot fathom God's word. It remains foreign to them.

When you are reading the Old Testament, keep in mind that it is about Jesus (e.g. Luke 24:27, 44), so look for promises about him. And as you read the Bible, remember what we are told it will do for us.

But as for you, continue in what you have learned and have firmly believed, knowing from whom you learned it and how from childhood you have been acquainted with the sacred writings, which are able to make you wise for salvation through faith in Christ Jesus. All Scripture is breathed out by God and profitable for teaching, for reproof, for correction, and for training in righteousness, that the man of God may be complete, equipped for every good work. (2 Timothy 3:14-17)

How I do it

It may be helpful for me to show you what I normally do when I read the Bible.

1. The first thing I do is pray that God will help me to understand the passage I am reading, with a view to obeying it. Sometimes when the Bible has corrected me, I am not always sure that I want to be obedient, so I pray that I will want to obey.

2. Next, I read the passage and try and think about what it means. I ask several questions:
    a. What does this passage tell me about God and the Lord Jesus?
    b. How should I respond to what I have read?
    c. Is there a promise in this passage?
    d. Is there a warning?

3. I pray that God will help me to put into practice in my life what I have just read.

Because of the sort of person I am, I keep a book where I write answers to these questions. You may not be like me, but I find this helps me to keep focused. I try and read the Bible each day at a time and place where I am not disturbed. For many people, this is really hard, but it is well worth the effort.

If I were just starting to read the Bible, I would begin by reading a Gospel. This helps me to realize that the Bible is about Jesus, and the Gospels tell us about him as clearly as any part of the Bible. I would then read the Acts of the Apostles, followed by Genesis.

I used to use Bible reading notes, which aim to tell me what the passage means. I often didn't find these notes particularly helpful, because I would read the passage, then read the notes, but I didn't think very much for myself about the text of the Bible. I thought the passage always meant what the notes said. I know this hasn't been the case for everyone, and many find notes to be a great help. Thank God we aren't all the same! Find a way that is right for you.

Whatever you do, think about the Bible as you read it.

Here is a sample page from my Bible reading notebook:

Date: 23.7.11

Passage: Romans 3:21-27

What does it tell me about God?
- God gives righteousness to those who have faith in Jesus (v. 22)
- God justifies me freely as a gift (v. 24)
- Jesus redeems me (v. 24)
- God sent Jesus as a sacrifice of atonement (v. 25)
- God is just when he forgives me because Jesus has taken the punishment my sins deserve (v. 27)

What does it tell me about myself?

- I need forgiveness (v. 22)
- I need to be justified and redeemed (v. 24)
- Jesus did that for me when he died in my place

My prayer:

Heavenly Father, thank you for your love in allowing Jesus to die in my place. Please help me to love you more and more.

If I did not know what 'a sacrifice of atonement' was, I would look it up in a Bible dictionary. If you don't have one of your own, there may be one in your church library, or you could look up the *New Bible Dictionary* online.

We have so many wonderful resources to help us understand the Bible, but the greatest resource is the Bible itself. There has never been a time in human history when we have had so many good translations of the Bible in English as we do today. I am sure that you own one.

What strange people we are! We can spend so much time wondering about God, but all the time we have a book in which God says everything we need to know to be godly. All we have to do is open it, read it and do what it tells us, and we will have rich fellowship with God. Why not give it a go for yourself?

APPENDIX

1 | Are the Gospels reliable histories?[1]

THROUGHOUT THIS BOOK, I HAVE assumed that Jesus is the Son of God and that the New Testament Gospels give reliable information about Jesus. But if the Gospels aren't really reliable, we cannot make a judgement on whether Jesus is the Son of God.

Several questions need to be asked.

Were the Gospels written by eyewitnesses?

Jesus' apostles were with him during the whole of his preaching and teaching career. They were eyewitnesses of his actions and words. Matthew, Mark, and John claim to be eyewitnesses. Luke may not have been a direct eyewitness, but he tells us that he went to eyewitnesses to compile an "orderly account" of the life and teachings of Jesus (Luke 1:3). There is a very old tradition that Mark's Gospel was dictated by the apostle Peter and written down by Mark.

It is clear that Matthew, Mark and Luke have the same material in several places. This suggests that they either spoke to the same eyewitnesses, or that they copied from each other, or from an older document which has now been lost. However, John does not tell many of the stories recorded in the other three Gospels, and he adds many others which they omit. Therefore, we have two independent accounts of Jesus' life. A good exercise would be to read Matthew, Mark and Luke and compare the Jesus we meet there with the Jesus we meet in John. I have done that exercise, and I am convinced that they are accounts of the same person.

Paul Barnett, former lecturer in New Testament History at Macquarie University and Sydney University, writes:

> While the Gospels have many distinctive features, they are in broad terms recognizable examples of history writers of their period. It is unhelpful and untrue to regard them merely as religious or theological works. They are also unmistakably historical in character. As historical sources of this period, they are just as valuable to the general historian as Josephus. Except, unlike Josephus, they are focused on one person and for a brief period.[2]

There are other ancient documents which claimed to be authentic Gospels, but which were rejected by the early church because they were known forgeries, or because their authorship could not be verified.

But weren't all the authors biased?

All of the authors of the Gospels were convinced Christians. They make no effort to conceal this. They tell us what evidence convinced them, and they invite us to see if we will not be convinced as we read them (e.g. John 20:31). Hardly anyone writes a book if they are not interested in the content. However, this does not mean they are necessarily inaccurate. Often, an interested party will take greater care to record an event accurately. I have always thought that someone who believed passionately in 'truth' is unlikely to knowingly falsify information.

When were they published?

Memories can last a long time, especially if the events are memorable.

Several years ago, I worked as an assistant minister at Moree, a small country town in northern New South Wales. I met a very elderly lady who told me, in a fair amount of detail, about making the 500 kilometre trek from Newcastle to Moree with her family when she was a small child. They brought all their possessions with them, and pioneered a property outside Moree.

Several years later, I met an elderly man who told me the same story. He was a boy from another family who had also made the trip. There was no doubt that the same events were being described. I don't doubt that the story had been told many times before. My mother's stories were told so often that we could prompt her when she forgot where she was up to!

In much the same way, the eyewitness accounts of Jesus' life were passed on orally for many years, and New Testament scholars agree that the Gospels were all available in their written form before the first century closed—perhaps within 30 years of Jesus' lifetime. There was plenty of opportunity for eyewitnesses to have objected and corrected misinformation, but we have no such evidence of this taking place.

Thirty years may seem a long time from the event until

it appears in final written form. But remember, the stories were very memorable, and they were being passed on orally throughout this time.

Have they been changed?

Just like most records from the time, we do not have any of the original documents of the New Testament. These were written in Greek on papyrus, and were copied as they became worn out.

The oldest full Gospel we have is estimated to have been written about 200-250 AD. This is called the Chester Beatty Biblical Papyri. There is a fragment of John's Gospel (John 18:31-33 and 37) housed in the John Rylands Library in Manchester. It is dated to about the middle of the second century. If we compare the difference in time between the oldest Gospel and copies from the fifth century, we can get a good indication that no substantial changes have been made.

If you are interested to read further on this subject, may I suggest you get a copy of *Is the New Testament History?* by Paul Barnett.[3] This book contains a valuable reading list for further investigation.

ENDNOTES

1. Much of the material in appendices 1 and 2 first appeared in John Chapman, *A Fresh Start*, Matthias Media, Kingsford, 1997.
2. Quoted in John Dickson, *Simply Christianity; Leader's Manual*, rev. edn, Matthias Media, Kingsford, 2003, p. 36.
3. Paul Barnett, *Is the New Testament History?*, Aquila Press, Sydney South, 2004.

2 | Is Jesus' claim to be God able to be substantiated?

So FAR, I HAVE ASSUMED THAT the claim of Jesus of Nazareth to be God is well-founded. He is an authoritative person who is to be heeded and obeyed. Here are my reasons for this belief.

There is no doubt that the Gospel writers think that Jesus repeatedly claimed to be equal with God. Here is an excellent example:

> This was why the Jews were seeking all the more to kill him, because not only was he breaking the Sabbath, but he was even calling God his own Father, making himself equal with God. (John 5:18)

The force of the present tense verbs in the original language is to show that not only was Jesus regularly breaking the Sabbath, but that he was repeatedly calling God his Father in such as way as to claim equality with God. To the Jews, such a claim was blasphemy, punishable by stoning. So, as John tells us, they tried to kill him.

Let me draw your attention to some more of his claims about himself.

The bread of life

Jesus said to them, "I am the bread of life; whoever comes to me shall not hunger, and whoever believes in me shall never thirst". (John 6:35)

Here, Jesus is claiming to be the one who can bring life satisfaction to anyone who comes to him. What an astonishing claim that is! Any family man knows how difficult that is with his family, let alone the entire world. Yet I know of thousands of people who claim that is exactly what faith in Jesus Christ has done for them.

The light of the world

Again Jesus spoke to them, saying, "I am the light of the world. Whoever follows me will not walk in darkness, but will have the light of life." (John 8:12)

What a truly astonishing statement he is making. He thinks he knows what life is about, and can enlighten any one who bothers to listen to him. It has never occurred to me to say that of myself! My friends would be uncontrollable with laughter.

The giver of eternal life

Jesus said to [the Samaritan woman], "Everyone who drinks of this water will be thirsty again, but whoever drinks of the water that I will give him will never be thirsty again. The water that I will give him will become in him a spring of water welling up to eternal life." (John 4:13-14)

Jesus believes that he can give eternal life to anyone who comes to him. This is a regular saying in John's Gospel (e.g. John 3:15; 5:24; 6:27, 40, 54; 10:28; 17:2-3).

The forgiver of sins

> And when Jesus saw their faith, he said to the paralytic, "Son, your sins are forgiven". (Mark 2:5)

This is the incident of the man brought to Jesus by his friends, who dig a hole through the roof and lower their paralyzed friend down so that Jesus may heal him. To their surprise, Jesus tells them that he has forgiven the man of his sins. This statement is yet another claim to be God. Only God—the chief offended party in all our sin—can pronounce our sins forgiven and give eternal life. There can be no doubt that Jesus thinks he is God in the flesh.

Lord and God

> "Your father Abraham rejoiced that he would see my day. He saw it and was glad." So the Jews said to him, "You are not yet fifty years old, and have you seen Abraham?" Jesus said to them, "Truly, truly, I say to you, before Abraham was, I am". (John 8:56-58)

This statement refers to a time when God called Moses to return to Egypt and to lead his people from slavery to the Promised Land. When Moses asks who he should say has sent him, God replies, "Say this to the people of Israel, 'I Am (or Yahweh) has sent me to you'" (Exodus 3:13-14). What is astonishing is that Jesus is claiming to be "I am"— the same person who sent Moses to free his people.

After his resurrection, when Thomas falls at Jesus' feet and declares, "[You are] my Lord and my God", Jesus makes no effort to stop him. Jesus believes that Thomas' summation is correct (John 20:24-29).

These outrageous claims, if not true, put Jesus into the category of the insane. If he is not God, then he cannot be a great moral teacher. He does not allow us that interpretation of himself. Listen to how C.S. Lewis sums it up:

> A man who was merely a man and said the sort of things Jesus said would not be a great moral teacher. He would either be a lunatic—on the level with the man who says he is a poached egg—or else he would be the Devil of Hell. You must make your choice. Either this man was, and is, the Son of God: or else a mad man or something worse. You can shut Him up for a fool; you can spit at Him and kill Him as a demon; or you can fall at His feet and call Him Lord and God, but let us not come with any patronizing nonsense about His being a great human teacher. He has not left that open to us. He did not intend to.[1]

Jesus the enigma

I have known many egotists, but never one like Jesus. They all seem to be totally self-centred, but Jesus is quite different. He is other-person-orientated. Did you notice that, in the shocking statements about himself, they were all directed at our welfare? He said, "I am the bread of life", so we can be satisfied. He said ,"I am the light of the world", so we can be enlightened. He is the forgiver of sins so that we can be at peace with God. He seems to be more concerned about me than I am myself! He says, "I am the judge of the entire world, so you need not fear the

Judgement Day. I am Lord and God, so you will know with whom you are dealing." What an enigma he is—the egotist who is deeply concerned for others!

He is so well balanced. He is angry when it is called for, and gentle when that is what's needed. He is so clever in answering questions. Do you recall the story of the woman caught in adultery (John 8:2-11)? They bring the woman to Jesus, and ask what should be done with her. It is an obvious set-up, but Jesus' answer is so clever: "Let him who is without sin among you be the first to throw a stone at her" (John 8:7). Notice how, with one sentence, he unmasks hypocrisy and does the right thing. From the greatest to the least, the people in the crowd all dribble away. Only Jesus and the woman are left. I would have been so excited, I would have asked her if she would like to have a drink with me. He, however, really cares about her:

> "Woman, where are they? Has no one condemned you?" She said, "No one, Lord". And Jesus said, "Neither do I condemn you; go, and from now on sin no more". (John 8:10-11)

I find myself saying, "I wish I had said that". He is so balanced, and so good.

I remember listening to an author on my radio as I lay in bed one night. He was asked if he made his characters good and bad. He said, "I try to make them real". It really is hard to make up a fictional character that is both good and real. However, when I see Jesus in action, I sense that I am in the presence of a really good man who is totally believable. Does he appear that way to you? Why not read the Gospels, and as you encounter this man, ponder if you think he is mad, or a deceiver—or is he really God after all?

His resurrection from the dead

All four Gospels tell of Jesus' resurrection from the dead. Jesus had foretold that this would happen (e.g. John 10:14-18), and it did. There were many eyewitnesses who testified to Jesus' resurrection. The apostles could not be shaken on this point. They had seen him alive again. They were so convinced that they would not change their story even when people thought they were mad—or, in some cases, even when it cost them their lives.

But what does the resurrection mean? That is what is important.

Jesus claimed to be Israel's Messiah. He claimed that he would sit on King David's throne forever. The resurrection shows that he is indeed who he claims to be: the Messiah.

You need to be convinced yourself. No-one can do the search for you. Is Jesus God? Then serve him as such. If he isn't, then don't bother.

There is one sure way to find out: read the Gospels for yourself.

Endnote
1. C.S. Lewis, *Mere Christianity*, Macmillan, New York, 1952, p. 40-41.

Feedback on this resource

We really appreciate getting feedback about our resources—not just suggestions for how to improve them, but also positive feedback and ways they can be used. We especially love to hear that the resources may have helped someone in their Christian growth.

You can send feedback to us via the 'Feedback' menu in our online store, or write to us at PO Box 225, Kingsford NSW 2032, Australia.

matthiasmedia

Matthias Media is an evangelical publishing ministry that seeks to persuade all Christians of the truth of God's purposes in Jesus Christ as revealed in the Bible, and equip them with high-quality resources, so that by the work of the Holy Spirit they will:

- abandon their lives to the honour and service of Christ in daily holiness and decision-making
- pray constantly in Christ's name for the fruitfulness and growth of his gospel
- speak the Bible's life-changing word whenever and however they can—in the home, in the world and in the fellowship of his people.

It was in 1988 that we first started pursuing this mission, and in God's kindness we now have more than 300 different ministry resources being used all over the world. These resources range from Bible studies and books through to training courses and audio sermons.

To find out more about our large range of very useful resources, and to access samples and free downloads, visit our website:

www.matthiasmedia.com

How to buy our resources

1. Direct from us over the internet:
  – in the US: www.matthiasmedia.com
  – in Australia and the rest of the world: www.matthiasmedia.com.au

2. Direct from us by phone:
  – in the US: 1 866 407 4530
  – in Australia: 1300 051 220
  – international: +61 2 9233 4627

> Register at our website for our **free** regular email update to receive information about the latest new resources, **exclusive special offers**, and free articles to help you grow in your Christian life and ministry.

3. Through a range of outlets in various parts of the world. Visit **www.matthiasmedia.com/contact** for details about recommended retailers in your part of the world, including www.thegoodbook.co.uk in the United Kingdom

4. Trade enquiries can be addressed to:
  – in the US and Canada: sales@matthiasmedia.com
  – in Australia and the rest of the world: sales@matthiasmedia.com.au

Also by John Chapman

Making the Most of the Rest of Your Life

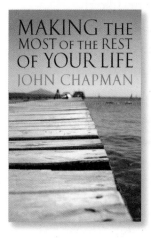

The Bible teaches that all people will die, and all will survive the grave and live either *with* Christ or *without* him in eternity. Evangelist John Chapman explores how we can know if this is true, and, if so, how to prepare for that eternity. This is a warm-hearted, good-humoured and challenging evangelistic book for 'seniors'. It explains how we can know about life after death, what the new creation will be like, and whether we can be sure of being part of it. (Large print!)

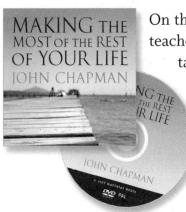

On this short DVD, well-known Bible teachers John Chapman and Tony Payne talk through the ideas in the book. It is an ideal alternative to the book for those who are less likely to read but more likely to watch an engaging discussion on TV. Run time: 22 minutes

FOR MORE INFORMATION OR TO ORDER CONTACT:

Matthias Media
Ph: 1300 051 220
Int: +61 2 9233 4627
Email: sales@matthiasmedia.com.au
www.matthiasmedia.com.au

Matthias Media (USA)
Ph: 1 866 407 4530
Int: +1 330 953 1702
Email: sales@matthiasmedia.com
www.matthiasmedia.com

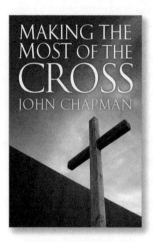
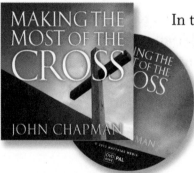

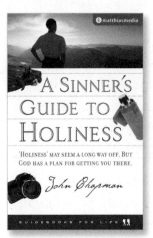
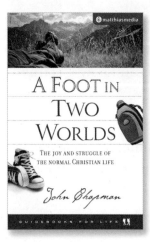